# FUNNY JOKES FOR 5 YEAR OLD KIDS

## 100+ Crazy Jokes That Will Make You Laugh Out Loud!

### Cooper the Pooper

© Copyright 2021 Cooper the Pooper - All rights reserved.

The content contained within this book may not be reproduced, duplicated or transmitted without direct written permission from the author or the publisher.

Under no circumstances will any blame or legal responsibility be held against the publisher, or author, for any damages, reparation or monetary loss due to the information contained within this book, either directly or indirectly.

**Legal Notice:**

This book is copyright protected. It is only for personal use. You cannot amend, distribute, sell, use, quote or paraphrase any part, or the content within this book, without the consent of the author or publisher.

**Disclaimer Notice:**

Please note the information contained within this document is for educational and entertainment purposes only. All effort has been executed to present accurate, up to date, reliable, complete information. No warranties of any kind are declared or implied. Readers acknowledge that the author is not engaged in the rendering of legal, financial, medical or professional advice. The content within this book has been derived from various sources. Please consult a licensed professional before attempting any techniques outlined in this book.

By reading this document, the reader agrees that under no circumstances is the author responsible for any losses, direct or indirect, that are incurred as a result of the use of the information contained within this document, including, but not limited to, errors, omissions or inaccuracies.

# TABLE OF CONTENTS

Table of Contents ........................................... 3

Introduction ................................................... 4

Chapter 1: Funny Jokes ............................. 6

Chapter 2: Crazy Jokes ............................ 18

Chapter 3: Laugh-out-Loud Jokes ........... 30

Chapter 4: Knock-Knock Jokes ................ 42

Chapter 5: Bonus Jokes ........................... 54

Final Words ............................................... 66

# INTRODUCTION

Well, hello there my little jokester — how are you today

I hope you are ready to have some laughs.

See, in your hand you have something that is very special. In fact, I would go as far as to say that it is super special. Yep, in your hand you hold a book that is full to the brim with hilarious jokes made just for five-year-old kids.

And trust me when I say these are not any old jokes. I spent years traveling the world going from country to country in search of the best jokes on the planet — and lucky for you, I think I found all of them.

These jokes cover every topic you can possibly imagine. From animals to dinosaurs to food to space, and then all the way back again, this book of jokes will have you in tears of laughter from start to finish.

And the best bit?

These jokes get funnier the more people you share them with.

Pick some of your favorites and tell your whole family (I bet even your grumpy old aunt will crack a smile). Save some of the best ones for your closest friends, or even take the book to school and have your whole classroom in stitches.

Just make sure that you take some time between jokes; otherwise you will be laughing so hard you might crack a rib.

So, what are you waiting for?

Turn the pages, dive on in, and start laughing at what can only be described as the perfect jokes for five-year-old kids.

# 1

## Where do cows go for entertainment?

- **The moo-vies.**

# 2

## What do you get when you cross a Labrador and a magician?

- **A Labracadabrador!**

## 3

What kind of facial hair does a moose have?

- A moostash.

## 4

How do you make an egg roll?

- Push it!

## 5

## What do you call a monkey at the North Pole?

- **Lost.**

## Where were pencils invented?

- **PENCIL-vania.**

## 7

Where do people go when they have two broken legs?

- **Nowhere!**

## 8

Which animal writes the best?

- **A pen-guin.**

## 9

## What is a cow's favorite place?

- A moo-seum.

## 10

## What's the best thing to put into a pie?

- Your teeth.

## What do you give a sick lemon?

- Lemon-aid.

## What is a snake's favorite subject?

- HISStory.

## 13

# How do ghosts greet each other?

- **"How do you boo?"**

## 14

# What did one elevator yell to the other?

- **I'm falling!**

# Why was the car so smelly?

- It had too much gas.

# Why did the ghost go to the hair salon?

- To make herself boo-tiful!

### 17

What toy is always in the bathroom?

- **The TOY-let!**

### 18

What do you call an old snowman?

- **Water.**

## 19

## What is the best day to go to the beach?

- **Sunday, of course!**

## 20

## What day do chickens hate?

- **Fry-day.**

# Why are chickens strong?

- **They egg-cersize!**

# What kind of key do you use to open a banana?

**A mon-key.**

# What did one ice cube say to the other?

- "I'm cooler than you!"

# What is a sheep's favorite superhero?

- Baaaaaaaatman.

# What's an owl's favorite toy?

- A hoo-la hoo-p.

# What do you call a sick eagle?

- Illegal.

## 5

# How do porcupines sound when they kiss?

- **Ow, ow, ouch!**

## 6

# Why didn't the five elephants under one umbrella get wet?

- **It wasn't raining!**

# Why can't dinosaurs vote?

- They're extinct!

# What do cats sing when they're celebrating?

- Three Blind Mice.

## 9

What did one snowman say to the other?

- **Have an ice day!**

## 10

If a door is not a door, then what is it?

- **A-jar.**

## 11

What do you call a guy lying on your doorstep?

• Matt.

## 12

What gifts are Santa giving out this year?

• Santa-tizers.

## 13

# What do you call a train that sneezes?

- **Achoo-choo train.**

## 14

# What do you call a gorilla with bananas in its ears?

- **Anything you like, he can't hear you.**

# Why do giraffes have such long necks?

- **Because they have smelly feet.**

# Why was six scared of seven?

- **Because seven eight nine.**

# What do snowmen do to lose weight?

- **Go to Florida.**

# Where do you find a dog with no legs?

- **Where you left him.**

# Why are pirates called pirates?

- **Because they ARRRRRR.**

# Why do dragons sleep during the day?

- **So they can fight knights.**

# How do you catch a squirrel?

- **Climb a tree and act like a nut.**

# What's orange and sounds like a parrot?

- **A carrot.**

## CHAPTER 3
# LAUGH-OUT-LOUD JOKES

## 1

## What do you call a fly without wings?

- **A walk.**

## 2

## What do elves learn at school?

- **The elf-abet.**

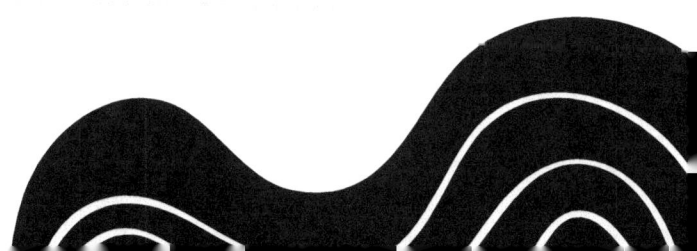

### 3

# What do you call a fairy that doesn't like to shower?

- **Stinkerbell.**

### 4

# What is a toad's favourite drink?

- **Croak-a-cola.**

## 5

# How do you start a teddy bear race?

- **Ready teddy go!**

## 6

# What do you call a rich elf?

- **Welfy.**

# 7

# When is it bad luck to meet a black cat?

- **When you're a mouse.**

# What shoes can you make out of bananas?

- **Slippers!**

## What do sea monsters eat?

- **Fish and ships!**

## What kind of witch do you find at the beach?

- **A sand-wich!**

## 11

What did the cat say when someone stepped on its tail?

- Me-OW.

## 12

Why are teddy bears never hungry?

- They're always stuffed!

## 13

# What do you call a cold bird in winter?

- **A brrr-d!**

## 14

# What do you call a huge ant?

- **Gi-ant.**

# What do you call a bear with no teeth?

- **A gummy bear.**

# What do you call a horse that lives in the house next to you?

- **A neeeeeeigh-bor.**

# What do you call a sheep with no legs?

- **A cloud.**

# What do you call a cow that plays the guitar?

- **A moo-sician!**

## 19

What's yellow and looks like pineapple?

• **A lemon with a new haircut.**

## 20

Why do birds fly south?

• **It's too far to walk.**

# Where does a rat go when it has a toothache?

- **To the rodentist.**

# What is a cat's favorite color?

- **Purrr-ple!**

# CHAPTER 4
# KNOCK-KNOCK JOKES

*Knock, knock!*
## Who's there?
**Hatch.**
## Hatch who?
**Bless you!**

*Knock, knock!*
## Who's there?
**Tank.**
## Tank who?
**You're welcome!**

## 3

*Knock, knock!*

# Who's there?

**Ketchup.**

# Ketchup who?

**Ketchup with me, and I'll tell you!**

## 4

*Knock, knock!*

# Who's there?

**Somebody too short t ring the doorbell!**

*Knock, knock!*

Who's there?

**Ice cream.**

Ice cream who?

**Ice cream if you don't let me inside!**

*Knock, knock!*

Who's there?

**Barbie.**

Barbie who?

**Barbie-q chicken!**

Knock, knock!
Who's there?
**Sing.**

Sing who?
**Whooo-ooo-ooo!**

Knock, knock!
Who's there?
**Wire.**

Wire who?
**Wire you asking me this?**

## 9

*Knock, knock!*

**Who's there?**

**Kanga.**

**Kanga who?**

**No, kangaroo!**

## 10

*Knock, knock!*

**Who's there?**

**I love.**

**I love who?**

**I don't know; why don't you tell me?!**

*Knock, knock!*

Who's there?

**Europe.**

Europe who?

**No, you're a poo!**

*Knock, knock!*

Who's there?

**Ali.**

Ali who?

**Alligator!**

## 13

*Knock, knock!*

## Who's there?

**Ruff.**

## Ruff who?

**Ruff, ruff It's your dog!**

## 14

*Knock, knock!*

## Who's there?

**Sir.**

## Sir who?

**Sir-prise! I have more jokes for you**

### 15

*Knock, knock!*

## Who's there?

**Jo.**

## Jo who?

**Jo King!**

### 16

*Knock, knock!*

## Who's there?

**Parrot.**

## Parrot who?

**Parrot who? Parrot who? Parrot who?**

## 17

Knock, knock!

**Who's there?**

**Says.**

**Says who?**

**Says me You looking for trouble?**

## 18

Knock, knock!

**Who's there?**

**Ozzie.**

**Ozzie who?**

**Ozzie you later, alligator!**

Knock, knock!
Who's there?
Boo.
Boo who?
Why are you so sad?

## 20

Knock, knock!
Who's there?
C.
C who?
You C me, but I can't see you.

## 21

*Knock, knock!*

### Who's there?

**Cows go.**

### Cows go who?

**No, cows go MOO!**

## 22

*Knock, knock!*

### Who's there?

**Cargo.**

### Cargo who?

**Car go, "Toot toot, vroom, vroom!"**

# 1

## What do ghosts like to eat in the summer?

- I scream.

# 2

## How do ghosts greet each other?

- "How do you boo?"

# What did one leaf say to another?

- I'm falling for you!

# What did one snowman tell the other?

- Let's chill out.

# How do you make a lemon drop?

- **Just let it fall.**

# Why was the baby strawberry crying?

- **Because her parents were in a jam.**

# What did the little corn say to the mama corn?

• **Where is popcorn?**

# What did one volcano say to the other?

• **I lava you!**

# How do we know that the ocean is friendly?

- **It waves!**

# What is a tornado's favorite game to play?

- **Twister!**

## 11

What do you call a funny mountain?

- Hill-arious.

## 12

Why couldn't the astronaut book a hotel on the moon?

- Because the moon was full.

# What did zero say to eight?

- **Nice belt!**

# Why do porcupines always win the game?

- **They have the most points.**

# Where do sheep go on vacation?

- **The Baaa-hamas.**

# What's a cow's favorite drink?

- **A smoooo-thie.**

## 17

# What falls in winter but never gets hurt?

- **Snow!**

## 18

# Why do bees hum?
- **They've forgotten the words.**

## 19

# What did one eye say to the other eye?

- **Between us, something smells!**

## 20

# Which hand is it better to write with?

- **Neither. It's better to write with a pencil!**

# FINAL WORDS

Before you go any further, I really wanted to thank you for reading my book.

I spent a very long time searching the planet for funny jokes so I could write this book — and nothing makes me happier than knowing that great kids like you are reading them.

But please remember, you are not done yet.

Yes, you have made it to the end of the book. But there is so much more to do.

It is time to go back through and pick out all your favorite jokes from this book and write them down on a special piece of paper. Then you are going to going to take that piece of paper and share those jokes with your friends and family.

After all, the only thing better than hearing a funny joke is telling a funny joke — so what are you waiting for?

**Go tell some jokes!**

www.ingramcontent.com/pod-product-compliance
Lightning Source LLC
Chambersburg PA
CBHW071408070526
44578CB00002B/517